CALLED

Mission Trip Devotions & Journal

Kathleen
Well

LENA WOOD

Standard
PUBLISHING
Bringing The Word to Life

Cincinnati, Ohio

Published by Standard Publishing, Cincinnati, Ohio

www.standardpub.com

Project editor: Lynn Lusby Pratt

Cover and interior design: The DesignWorks Group

Printed in: China

ISBN 978-0-7847-2284-8

14 13 12 11 10 09 08   9 8 7 6 5 4 3 2 1

YOU'VE BEEN CALLED

You're going on a mission trip! There's so much on your to-do list. In the hurry and excitement, don't forget Jesus.

Of course, you won't forget him! But remember the comparison you sometimes hear—that there's a difference between just knowing *about* Jesus and actually *knowing* him? One of the biggest hazards of ministry is getting lost in the details of the Lord's work and losing the real focus: Jesus himself. The purpose of this book is to keep you close to Jesus while you prepare to go into all the world. Your trip is *for* him *and* with him.

The editorial staff for this project has worked hard to prepare these devos for you. We adore Jesus with our whole hearts and care deeply about getting his good news out—through you! Content Editor Dale Reeves was a short-termer on trips to Haiti and Mexico and risks life and limb on a weekly basis, leading a band of restless savages (young guys) in his home church. Detail Queen Lynn Pratt was a missionary in Japan for ten years and hangs out with "the internationals" at conventions all over the country. Writer and part-time blonde Lena Wood is a multi-short-termer with a prayer map of the world on her office wall and a passion for traveling light. Frankly, we'd all love to chuck our day jobs long enough to go with you!

You hold in your hands two weeks' worth of devos plus one. There's a lot to digest in every devo, so feel free to start early and take even more time if you can. But definitely finish up the whole book before you go. Here's what you'll find:

- Lots of spiritual nourishment
- Lined journal pages for writing your thoughts and prayers
- Blank pages for sketching and dreaming. Or if you're planning to trek in Nepal, do jungle missions in Nicaragua, or end up in a poorly supplied rest stop in Nebraska . . . you have fifteen sheets of free toilet paper!

Scattered throughout the book are a few special features to help along the way: Prayer (focus, guides, stories), Travel (tips, facts, advisories), and Culture (shocks, stats, clues).

OK, you've got your to-do list and your devos. Get going, beloved of God. You've been *Called*!

NOTE: Some of the names and locations mentioned in this book have been changed, and the details of some stories represent compilations.

THE CALL

How did you get the call—from a church bulletin?

Short-Term Mission Trip: Volunteers Needed

(Hmm . . . sounds interesting. I've been wanting to do one of those.)

Did you get the call from your minister or Bible study leader? "Hey (your name here), we have an opportunity to put hands and feet on the gospel. We'd love to have you join us."

(He's right. It's time to ramp up my commitment to Jesus, step out on faith.)

Did the call come because a Scripture like Romans 10:13-15 spoke to you with new relevance?

(How can they call on Jesus if they don't believe? How can they believe if they don't hear? How can they hear without someone to tell them . . . someone like me?)

Or did His Majesty speak into your mind and heart? "You need to go there."

(Wha—?)

"You need to go."

(But how? I mean, what about—?)

"You need to go."

How *were* you called?

Perhaps the call didn't exactly come from a deep yearning, a holy tug at your soul. Think honestly about it. Maybe you signed up for less than noble reasons:

- It sounded more fun than your last family vacation with Aunt Lulu.
- You'd feel more spiritual if you did some mission work.
- It's a cheap way to get out of the country.
- You like traveling and want to hit a few new ports before you die.
- You've been looking for a way to spice up a bland season of your life.

Jonah's Wail

Motives not the best? No matter. Jonah's motives were way past stinkeroo. He didn't like those pagan Ninevites. In his mind they deserved the Hell they were going to get. He hated the idea of mission work so badly that he ran.

But Yahweh looked with an eye of mercy toward Nineveh. With his holy will fixed on a naive prophet (who thought he could go AWOL from the Almighty), God pulled the great fish fiasco. Jonah's options were narrowed to one: repent 'n' go.

So Jonah went. He grudgingly preached. A city repented. Disaster was forestalled.

Jonah's selfish wail in Jonah 4:3 might as well say, "Oh, just kill me now!"

Perhaps the prophet's story has been preserved for us so we'll see that God can use even prejudiced, disobedient, self-centered sneaks—with startling success.

The call for all believers to go into all the world has been echoing for two thousand years. You don't need a new, specific call—a bolt from the blue. Every believer knows he should go and teach (Matthew 28:18-20). So you've put your hand to the plow. Don't turn back.

Packing Logistics

After your call, the questions came: *How many clothes should I take? Cash or credit? Luggage or backpack?*

Jesus' answer: none of the above.

A typical modern-day list of essentials for a mission trip might include: a week's worth of outfits, extra shoes, communication tools (stationery, cell phone, address list), transportation tickets, money (cash, traveler's checks, credit card), backpack, hair products, shaving kit, bedding. Digital camera. Travel games. Sanitary hand wipes (an absolute necessity in Haiti and other developing countries!). Water filter . . .

Jesus told his short-termers no. And since he *created* short-term missions, he should know. Read Matthew 10:1-20. Jesus called his disciples and sent them out on foot to neighboring towns for the short haul. What were the essentials? Spiritual authority, power to heal, a simple sermon, a generous spirit, peace, discretion, innocence, caution, the leading of the Holy Spirit, and courage.

No worries about weight limits there.

Jesus' list bears little resemblance to today's typical

what-to-take lists—even those offered by seasoned mission organizations.

If you're leaving soon and haven't stockpiled some peace and courage, if you don't have a testimony about what Jesus means to you or a heart open to the Holy Spirit's surprising directives . . . that'd be a good place to start.

But be greatly encouraged. The Lord specializes in impossible missions with clueless disciples: a few fishermen, a tax guy, even a traitor in the bunch pilfering the funds. With them he changed the world. If this is your first trip and you're a little edgy, you're in good company; so were the clueless called ones.

The first Christians—and myriads since—set out with little or nothing but Jesus' list. Matthew 8:20 ("the Son of Man has no place to lay his head") sounds like Jesus himself didn't even always have a designated place to stay. So what are you thinking about taking with you?

Jesus' instructions reflect what he said elsewhere. Don't be concerned about what you will eat or drink or wear. Seek the kingdom of God first, and all the rest will be provided (Matthew 6:33). It's not some platitude. Jesus meant it literally. Take heart, even in your lack of preparation. With a ragtag band of newbies outfitted with his list, Jesus saw great results: "They went out and preached that people should repent. They drove out many demons and anointed many sick people with oil and healed them" (Mark 6:12, 13).

It's an adventure: an undertaking of a hazardous, questionable, daring, or exciting nature. But Jesus will be with you.

Still determined to take luggage? hair products? cash? That's OK. You're probably going much farther than Jesus' first short-termers. Just keep in mind that spiritual prep is most important. Travel light. Don't get so focused on creature comforts that you put off getting your spirit outfitted for service. That way, if your worldly possessions should get lost or stolen, you'll still have what you really need.

IN GOD'S HANDS

Mission recruits often get worried looks from loved ones, even when they're just going into their own inner city. "Will you be safe there? What about the dangers?"

When Russell and Gertrude Morse set out for Tibet in 1921, some well-meaning church members worried about their taking a newborn to a "wild, robber-infested country." They warned, "If anything happens to that baby, God will hold you responsible and bring judgment on you" (*The Dogs May Bark, But the Caravan Moves On* by Gertrude Morse).

TRAVEL

Well, times they are a-changin'. Many countries worldwide are now safer, with lower crime rates than America. Ireland, for instance, and Denmark, Japan, New Zealand, and Norway. Check out www.globalin cidentmap.com. Look at the reports of suspicious packages, sabotage, eco-terrorism, kidnapping attempts, etc. The threats are always present in our country. Even our children are at greater risk than

ever here. Murders in our high schools. Child moles-
tation in lofty rectories . . . Would you be in more danger in Uzbekistan, Jamaica, South Africa, Colombia,
Somalia, or Indonesia? Maybe not. The evil one isn't
restricted by time zones and borders. Dangers lurk in
Hometown, U.S.A. We've just gotten used to them.

What everyday dangers lurk in your area? Tornadoes,
floods, West Nile virus, drugs, predators, poverty, fault
lines, forest fires, copperheads, or those 7-inch-long and
totally creepy black centipedes that won't die even when
you chop their heads off and put them in a sealed jar for
several days? (Oklahoma, 1984, youth mission trip).

Danger is everywhere. The works of Satan ravage
billions by hunger and disease. Worldwide, 100 million
homeless children fight for their lives—yes, 100 million,
according to Compassion International. Two of the
world's "great" religions bow to demonic idols. An
estimated 27 million people around the globe are slaves.

Spiritual Battle

Spiritually speaking, you're just leaving one war zone
for another. Ever since the Garden of Eden, when the

first couple gave in to the serpent's offer—"You will be like God"—there has been hostility between him and humankind (Genesis 3:4-15). And this hostility is a good thing actually. God forbid that there would be harmony between the serpent and God's children!

Using militant terms about our faith may not be politically correct, but the Scriptures don't shy away from spiritual warfare. Here are a few examples for you to dwell on:

"The LORD is a warrior; the LORD is his name" (Exodus 15:3).

"When they chose new gods, war came to the city gates" (Judges 5:8).

"David said to the Philistine, 'You come against me with sword and spear and javelin, but I come against you in the name of the LORD Almighty'" (1 Samuel 17:45).

"Too long have I lived among those who hate peace. I am a man of peace; but when I speak, they are for war" (Psalm 120:6, 7).

"Wisdom is better than weapons of war" (Ecclesiastes 9:18).

"The LORD will march out like a mighty man, like a warrior he will stir up his zeal; with a shout he will raise the battle cry and will triumph over his enemies" (Isaiah 42:13).

"The end will come like a flood: War will continue until the end, and desolations have been decreed" (Daniel 9:26).

"Do not suppose that I have come to bring peace to the earth. I did not come to bring peace, but a sword" (Matthew 10:34).

"I see another law at work in the members of my body, waging war against the law of my mind and making me a prisoner of the law of sin at work within my members" (Romans 7:23).

"Our struggle is not against flesh and blood, but against the rulers, against the authorities, against the powers of this dark world and against the spiritual forces of evil in the heavenly realms" (Ephesians 6:12).

"We know that we are children of God, and that the whole world is under the control of the evil one" (1 John 5:19).

"Abstain from sinful desires, which war against your soul" (1 Peter 2:11).

"And there was war in heaven. . . . The dragon was enraged at the woman and went off to make war against the rest of her offspring—those who obey God's commandments and hold to the testimony of Jesus" (Revelation 12:7, 17).

"I saw heaven standing open and there before me was a white horse, whose rider is called Faithful and True. With justice he judges and makes war" (Revelation 19:11).

We Win

The end of the Book tells us that we're fighting for the right side. As you prepare to leave on your trip, the evil one may shake you by the shoulders and say, "You can't do this. You'll never make it!" But press ahead.

As you think about spiritual battles you may have to face, what things concern you?

Why do you have confidence that God is in control?

While you are in the world, you will have trouble. Jesus didn't promise world peace in the sense we hear it talked about. (Sorry to burst your bubble.) No place is safe. But there is peace in Christ (John 16:33). And in his hands you are always safe.

ALL NEWS IS GOOD NEWS

Suffering comes in all sizes. Take my last flight home from the mission field—please! It was a thirteen-hour flight. I always try to get a window seat; I love looking out at the world to pass the time. But on this flight I was assigned a center seat. The man in the window seat slammed the shade down at takeoff and slept the whole way, except to eat his meals. In silence. Not much of a conversationalist.

My overhead light didn't work; I could barely read. My headphones didn't work. I watched silent movies with no subtitles.

In the dark. For thirteen hours.

The man on my right slept the whole way too, and—how shall I put this delicately?—he had "digestive problems." I stared straight ahead into the gloom and tried not to inhale. For thirteen hours.

OK, so it wasn't ten years in a Turkish prison, a diet of bread and water, and a firing squad. But I'm a short-termer! I wasn't built to suffer!

The Good News

Some people say that for a writer there's no such thing as bad news. It's all fodder for the next article, the next illustration, the next adventure plot. The more crises, the better. Those impossible people in a writer's real life show up later in fiction as quirky, but authentic, characters. Yessir, troubles are our bread and butter. So bring on the tragedy, we say. We don't mind!

Of course we *do* mind. But there's a silver lining to every writer's storm cloud, and it's called good material. Your stories of inconvenience, drama, and suffering will be pure gold. Discipline yourself to write every day. You won't regret it.

TRAVEL

OK, maybe some experiences *are* best avoided—like getting lost. Always carry the address and telephone number of the place you're staying (and possibly a map), so that someone can help you find your way back. In some cities you can't go around the block because there are no blocks. The saying "You can't get there from here" may have originated on a mission trip.

Some troubles we cause ourselves. There was the missionary who thought the $100 bouquet left on her porch was a thank-you gift. She cut the flowers and put them on display in her house. They weren't for her. A new missionary once told her doctor in broken Japanese, "I think I'm a carrot!" She was trying to say, "I think I'm pregnant" (*ninshin*=pregnant, *ninjin*=carrot; too close to call).

Some drama is caused by others. I have a folder in my files from early in ministry labeled Church Members from Hell. This was back when I naively thought that troublesome events in ministry were rare phenomena. Yeah. Naive. I've since learned.

My CMfH file includes a newsletter from the late '70s warning the churches: *The Women are Coming! The Women are Coming! Watch and Pray!!* There's also a story of a man who asked me to sing a duet with him for worship service, then filmed it to make his wife jealous. I call that story "Mr. Strangelove." And did you hear the one about the two elders who nearly got into a fistfight over which way a door in the fellowship hall should swing? I call it "Extreme Makeover: Fellowship Hall Edition."

Years ago, missionaries received care packages from the States that included used tea bags and 3-way lightbulbs with two of the settings burned out. Used tea bags and burned-out bulbs? Garbage shipped six thousand miles! Such true horror stories have been circulated around the globe as examples of how *not* to treat your missionary. Whoever sent those "gifts" . . . I'm tempted to add their stories to my CMfH file.

As for your mishaps and struggles, write them all down: the quicksand, typhoons and earthquakes, the child who steals your wallet, the sprained wrist, the anti-American demonstrators, missed flights, lost passport, strange food, demon encounters, ridiculous rules, agonizing waits.

CULTURE

Take a good look at some of the things that you think would qualify as inconvenient or suffering; for example, not having meat in your meals for a week. In India (or Indiana for that matter), your host might not be able to serve everything you're used to. Transportation might be uncomfortable—and possibly four-legged. Are you aware of the great sacrifices your hosts are making to be able to house you and provide for you? If they can live with less *every* day, can't you enjoy doing so for a *few* days?

An Adventure with God

Be courageous. Don't complain—especially to your team leader or the missionary—unless the problem is of an overwhelming nature. Your leaders have way more pressure than you might imagine. Put your troubles in writing instead. Use lots of adjectives. And of course, tell it to Jesus. The good stuff and the bad.

PRAYER

Start the habit now. Talk with the Lord about your hopes for your upcoming trip, as well as some of the complaints you already have.

If your trip is easy, comfortable, and predictable, it won't be a real adventure, will it? If you come back relaxed and refreshed, it's likely you failed. Your journal should contain words like *exhausted, frustrated, tension-in-the-air-so-thick-you-could-cut-it-with-a-knife, chowderhead, ankle-deep, satanic, crowded, nauseated,* and *disoriented*.

Tribulation worketh patience . . . and maketh great dinner conversation once you're back home.

You might also plan to keep a quotes page. Write down the funny, strange things your teammates say when they're tired or not thinking clearly. Note some plays on words from the culture. When my 2003 mission trip crew discovered a milky drink named Qoo, one member started saying, "Don't cry over spilt Qoo." Hilarious.

And save the treasured moments in writing too:

- Hanging out in the kitchen until midnight, talking about God.
- The speedy train ride through the mountains.
- First view of the bay.
- First person you bonded with on the field.
- The crowded café where you found yourself yelling about Jesus.

- The child who clung to you.
- The mother who cried.
- The missionary's backstory, his trials and tribs.

"We know that in all things [*even the troubles*] God works for the good of those who love him, who have been called according to his purpose" (Romans 8:28). This is never more true than when you're working 24/7 for God. Get it in writing. It's all good news.

You can start writing now. As you've been preparing for your trip, what God appointments, coincidental happenings, or funny situations have occurred?

ANYTHING TO DECLARE?

Back in my Bible college days, a fellow student and daughter of a missionary told stories of smuggling Bibles into Communist Russia. It was pretty exciting stuff, the subterfuge of tucking Bibles into one's coat or girdle (it was the late '60s—we wore girdles then) and praying hard that the Communist guards wouldn't notice.

Vanita Dulin's spiritual spy stories were exciting to us sheltered, corn-fed Midwesterners who thought of secret agents in terms of Hollywood's *Get Smart* and James Bond. What Vanita didn't share with us at the time were the horrors: humiliating strip searches, nearly being banned from her beloved Romania, the fear of never seeing dear friends again, the worry that her own mistakes would bring down persecution on the heads of the nationals. She also didn't relate to us how she hid in a restroom, tearing and chewing up pages of forbidden literature before she flushed them down the toilet.

She did what she had to do, learning the rules as she went along.

On a lighter note . . . Someone I know (name withheld to protect my mother) once smuggled a country ham into a foreign country so her loved ones on the mission field could have an authentic taste of home. This might have been illegal; it's perishable foodstuff. She didn't ask; we didn't tell.

Don't try this on your trip.

TRAVEL

Security is tight worldwide. If your trip takes you across borders, you may have to answer the question "Do you have anything to declare?" In the airport you'll have to take off your shoes and walk through a scanner. You may have to open your luggage for inspection. You won't be allowed large bottles of liquid or tubes of gel in your carry-on. Be cooperative. And don't say the word *bomb*, even in jest.

The former USSR has opened up considerably since the '60s. The Iron Curtain and the Berlin Wall have come down. But in some cultures it's still illegal to import and declare the gospel. And even when permitted by law, you and your good news may not be welcome. One mission team to India was working in the Ladakh area, backpacking into the mountains to share the gospel. Some villagers tried to stone them.

Yes, stoning. In the twenty-first century.

On a Mission from God

Jesus' Great Commission takes precedence over temporal law or personal safety. When challenged, Peter and John said to the Sanhedrin, "We cannot help speaking about what we have seen and heard" (Acts 4:20). Paul admonished Timothy, "Preach the Word; be prepared in season and out of season" (2 Timothy 4:2). "In season and out of season" means when Jesus is popular and when he's not, when you're safe and when you're not.

What do you want to declare about your life in Christ? Need help putting it simply? Formulate a mission statement. An easy way is to choose a verb, an object, a method, and a purpose. Here are a few samples to help you complete the sentence: My mission in life is to . . .

- **verb**—heal, produce, teach, manage, inspire
- **object**—children, paper products, foreigners, an office, adults

- **method**—hospital, family business, English, part-time, Sunday school
- **purpose**—ministry to families, provision of family, sharing the Bible, staying home with children, learning God's Word

The first mission statement from the above lists would be: "My mission in life is to help heal children in a hospital setting in order to minister to families." The second would be: "to produce paper products in a family business in order to provide for my family."

Your mission statement at this time in your life may be occupation-related or ministry-driven, whatever God has called you to. If you feel you've lost sight of God's original design for your life, think back to your childhood. What were your aspirations then? It's never too late to regroup. Try your hand at writing your mission statement here.

Next is your testimony, your love story. How would you complete this thought: I love Jesus because . . .

Explain in a few sentences either how the Lord brought you from darkness to light or how you have been blessed by knowing Christ from the beginning of your life.

Maybe you're not going to preach or teach on this trip. You may be a builder, a doctor, a weed puller . . . Whatever your job, please don't leave your field without sharing your heart and testimony with at least one person. The people you meet don't need Genesis to Revelation . . . just yet. They do need to hear the name of Jesus, spoken in love.

What's your testimony? Write it here.

When the airport security person asks, "Do you have anything to declare?" he or she will be referring to things like weapons, live plants and animals, contraband country ham. The proper answer is "No."

But tucked away in your heart, you most certainly *do* have something to declare: what you're doing with your life and what Jesus means to you.

Vanita Dulin has been to eighty countries since the '60s. Like Peter and John, she didn't stop declaring. And one young man on that team to Ladakh is going back as soon as he can—to keep spreading the Word.

So traveler, what do you have to declare?

PRAYER

As you continue to make preparations for your mission trip, talk to God about your mission statement. Have you asked him if your statement is in line with his will for your life? Speak with him also about the testimony he has given you. Give the Father thanks that you have something to declare.

JUST BE YOURSELF...
NO, WAIT!

Compare the average Japanese person to the average white, middle-class American. Japanese are darker, shorter, thinner (sumo wrestlers excepted), quieter, cleaner, more reserved, very polite, and great gift-givers. So the typical U.S. citizen would be ... what—pale, tall, fat (runway models excepted), loud, dirty, aggressive, rude, and stingy? Yikes. There may be a grain of truth to the "ugly American" stereotype.

Many U.S. citizens are a bit insulated from the rest of the world. Often out of touch with exotic, foreign customs, we may tend to judge everything by American standards. Other countries, we say, drive on the "wrong" side of the road. Their food is "bad." They dress "funny."

CULTURE

In fact, we're all a little strange. Look at these tidbits of culture from www.worldcitizensguide.org:

- In Algeria, the traditional symbol of manhood is a mustache.
- In Belgium, talking with your hands in your pockets is considered rude.
- In El Salvador, it's rude to point with the index finger.
- In Guatemala, the bigger the hand motion used in hailing a cab, the longer the distance you have to go.
- Indonesians don't like the tops of their heads touched.
- Nepalese think that wanting personal space or to spend time by yourself is strange.
- Pakistani men are often seen holding hands, but men and women holding hands may be frowned upon.
- In Romania, you should call only very close friends or family members by their first names.
- For Tunisians, time is relative; tomorrow could mean next week.
- In Uganda, taking a gift from someone with both hands shows appreciation.

- In Zimbabwe, respect is shown by lowering yourself. People don't stand when their superiors enter
  the room.

TRAVEL

Poland and Thailand (and possibly other countries)
have "wet" holidays when people suddenly throw
buckets of cold water on each other for no reason.
You may want to check out such things, and dress
accordingly.

If you've traveled to a different culture before, what
customs seemed odd to you?

Worst Offenders

To some around the world, we Americans don't
sit right, wave right, eat right, or dress right. In one

culture the ways we blow our noses, bathe, and use the restroom are disgusting. In another we're way too frou-frou about such things. Still others think we're soft or greedy or immoral or pushy. Less than a century ago, we were "foreign devils" in the Orient. How do you overcome that stereotype? As an American short-termer, you may have some bitter pills to swallow.

CULTURE

Missionary Kim Daniels, as a new recruit to Ghana, overheard her native coworker say, "Missionaries are the worst offenders when it comes to working with the local church." The complaint sprang from Americans coming to a foreign culture with their money and ideas on how things should be done, with little regard for a culture where people look at life very differently. The comment was a stinging blow for the American missionary, but one she took to heart.

A few hard truths: People may be resentful of your presence. Or something you do in innocence or ignorance may highly offend them.

On the other hand, they may respond to your invitation to Christ simply because they think it's the polite thing to do. Perhaps the local minister has been working for years; and then in response to this short-termer's brief visit, here comes a flock of responses. You're thrilled. You have great stories of success to take home. But when you leave, so do the converts—back to their old ways. The missionary ends up more disappointed and exhausted than before you came.

Some nationals may come to see you only out of curiosity . . . or hoping to get money . . . or even to find an American spouse. The short-termer's heartstrings are tugged, gifts are given with best intentions. Bibles offered generously sometimes end up sitting on a shelf; what the person really wanted was money. And we have to be understanding— who wants a book when his kids are hungry? And who wouldn't take unusual measures to feed his family?

Veteran missionary Garland Bare gives several valuable insights into the culture gap ("Why Don't They Love Us?" *Christian Standard*, 04/21/02):

- While some poor people will appreciate your help, others may resent your comparative wealth. Live modestly. And don't complain.
- Your generosity may be seen as having an ulterior motive, and viewed with suspicion. Work quietly.
- Darkness hates the light, and there's nothing you can do about that. If you are working in a demonic stronghold surrounded by nonbelievers, there will be resistance. Just keep shining.

Keep Shining

Let's conclude on a positive note. There are two sides to every story: Americans are also appreciated worldwide for their optimism, creativity, music, sports, resourcefulness, movies, self-sacrifice, independence, and pioneer spirit.

Paul and Silas were treated like gods in one place, stoned and imprisoned in the next. You might experience the gamut. Prepare your heart. Carefully watch your bounds. Count any success you have as an extension of the local minister's or veteran missionary's work. Give God all the glory.

Take time to evaluate yourself. "Do not think of yourself more highly than you ought, but rather think of yourself with sober judgment, in accordance with the measure of faith God has given you" (Romans 12:3).

How do you exemplify Christ? How do you need to prepare your heart and spirit as you head into a foreign culture?

PRAYER

Spend some time today talking to God about your attitude and motivation.

WHAT CAN YOU BUY
WITH A WIDOW'S MITE?

My family was touring the Ink & Blood exhibit, a traveling museum that tells the story of the Bible. On display were clay tablets, tiny scraps of Dead Sea Scrolls, and illuminated parchments from the Middle Ages, as well as Bibles from every era. We heard stories of brave men and women who suffered unimaginable torture because of their love for God's Word and for the people who needed to hear it. Some persecutors burned the "heretics" at the stake instead of beheading them, so they could not be accused of "shedding blood."

Handcrafted, illuminated Bibles in today's economy would cost a year's wage to produce. So many gave so much. Some gave all. I felt new appreciation for my collection of Bibles—*KJV, NIV, New Century,* electronic, and so on—which had cost me so little.

Afterwards, we strolled through the gift shop with its offerings of books and other souvenirs. Something caught my eye: a tiny, corroded chip of metal encased in glass. It was a widow's mite.

Sacrifice Observed

The little story is in Mark 12. Jesus was teaching in the temple, blatantly warning the crowd about the teachers of the law (who were likely standing right there listening). "They like to walk around in flowing robes and be greeted in the marketplaces, and have . . . places of honor at banquets. They devour widows' houses and for a show make lengthy prayers. Such men will be punished most severely" (vv. 38-40).

Then Jesus sat down to watch as people put their offerings into the temple treasury. Rich folks threw in bags o' money. Then here came a woman in black, a widow. She put in two small copper coins worth a fraction of a penny. Jesus praised her to his disciples: "I tell you the truth, this poor widow has put more into the treasury than all the others. They all gave out of their wealth; but she, out of her poverty, put in everything—all she had to live on" (vv. 43, 44).

The mite on display in the glass case was the size of a fingernail, paper thin, jagged, and black from age. But how cool would it be to own a coin from Jesus' time! What a great object lesson for a children's sermon! I wanted it. Then I saw the sign above the display: Widow's mite—$29.95.

I hadn't counted on two thousand years of inflation.

Exchange Rate

TRAVEL

Your money may be worth more or less where you're going. What's the average wage there? If you go to Ireland or Singapore, costs will be comparable to the U.S. But in most countries your daily wage is a fortune. Check out www.success-and-culture.net.

The price of that widow's mite—$29.95—would keep a child in Kenya alive for a month. I couldn't escape the irony. I didn't buy it.

Count up the total estimated cost of your trip. Divide by $30. That's how many children could survive for a month if you were to stay home and contribute that money to child sponsorship. So let's be frank. If you're going just to paint a house or dig a well, wouldn't it be wiser to send the money, to provide wages so folks there could earn a salary digging or painting? If you're going for educational purposes—to teach English—maybe you should just send a laptop with ESL software.

It's more complicated than that, isn't it? How much is your presence worth? The love of Jesus flowing directly through you—how much is that worth?

How much is the gospel worth to the lost? Jesus asked the question, "What good is it for a man to gain the whole world, and yet lose or forfeit his very self?" (Luke 9:25). How much would you pay to spend eternity in Heaven with the Lord and your loved ones? How much to escape Hell?

Exactly. Jesus didn't give an answer either, because there is no answer.

Jesus said, "Go." So go. Don't back down. He saw in the widow's mite a different kind of exchange rate. A little given in love is a fortune to him.

Sacrifices Made

Relatively speaking, your trip costs you little. You probably won't have to close out your bank account and sell off furniture. Or maybe you will. Either way, it's right that it costs you something. King David said, "I will not sacrifice to the LORD my God burnt offerings that cost me nothing" (2 Samuel 24:24). What kind of sacrifice costs you nothing? No sacrifice at all.

TRAVEL

And speaking of sacrifice, consider dipping into the spending money you plan to take, so you can buy supplies for the missionaries you'll be visiting. Could they use Bible story coloring books, medical supplies, things for the office, chocolate cake mixes or other nonperishable favorite foods? Another possible sac-rifice: if you're traveling to an impoverished area, the clothes you pack for yourself might be something you can leave behind when your trip ends.

What will the investment of your widow's mite be worth in spiritual returns? Spend some time today thinking about that.

LOVE BY LISTENING

Hopefully, you've worked on your testimony, not just for the mission field but also for any opportunity before, during, or after the trip. You want to be ready to say the right thing when the time comes. Your words will have weight. But what you *say* on the field may not be as important as what you *hear*.

Listening is an act of love. If this is true, then Romeo's got nothing on my dad. Mom has always had the gift of gab—retelling favorite stories, handing out detailed instructions, and offering lengthy warnings. Mom does most of the talking, while Dad balances out their sixty-two-year marriage by being a man of few words. Here are some examples of his quippy wisdom:

When my sister and I used to play with our food, we didn't get the typical sermon about starving children in Africa, which would have been lost on preschoolers. Dad commanded, "Don't make goop."

On family vacations, when asked where we should eat, stop, or sightsee, Dad's invariable answer was, "Whatever suits the rest."

On Mom's giving blood at a local drive: "Whoever gets *her* blood, they'll sure see a change!"

On why he trusted his cancer surgeon: "He knows *him* too."

A final case in point. Mom's always been concerned about germs. She gave endless instructions on keeping our hands clean, how to turn on the kitchen faucet to wash dirty hands without soiling the clean handle; or conversely, in the case of using a public restroom, how one shouldn't touch the dirty faucet handle to turn off the water after washing one's hands, thereby re-dirtying the clean hands. What to do? How to handle the handle dilemma? Mom would demonstrate using a knuckle or an elbow, or use a piece of paper towel to turn the faucet on . . . or off . . .

Dad's concise advice: "Or use your foot."

The Word on Words

The Bible has a lot to say about talking and listening:

"When words are many, sin is not absent, but he who holds his tongue is wise. The tongue of the righteous is choice silver, but the heart of the wicked is of little value. The lips of the righteous nourish many, but fools die for lack of judgment" (Proverbs 10:19-21).

"With my lips I recount all the laws that come from your mouth" (Psalm 119:13).

"Take words with you and return to the LORD. Say to him, 'Forgive all our sins and receive us graciously, that we may offer the fruit of our lips'" (Hosea 14:2).

"Take note of this: Everyone should be quick to listen, slow to speak and slow to become angry. . . . Do not merely listen to the word, and so deceive yourselves. Do what it says" (James 1:19, 22).

Read James 3 and jot down a few ideas about how and when to speak. Stash those precepts in your heart too.

Meditate on how often the Lord loves you by listening. "Give ear to my words, O LORD, consider my sighing. Listen to my cry for help, my King and my God, for to you I pray. In the morning, O LORD, you hear my voice; in the morning I lay my requests before you and wait in expectation" (Psalm 5:1-3).

What things has God heard from you lately?

Show, Don't Tell

Show love by listening. Ask questions about people's families. Inquire about the history of the area you're working in, or about sports, hobbies, ancestors, geography, work, politics, religion. Soak it in. Learn a lot. If you're training with a team, start by listening to them now. Not with the goal of getting your turn to speak later, but as an act of genuine affection and interest.

My friend Saundra has this message on her phone: "People don't care how much you know until they know how much you care." We all need that reminder occasionally, don't we? People will know much more about you than your stats or your opinions. They'll know how much you care.

CULTURE

A picture really is worth a thousand words, especially if there's a language barrier. Photos facilitate conversation. So do carry along a mini album to show photos of your family (dressed modestly). You may not have to say a word about your love; people will see the glow on your face, the sparkle in your eye. Include a few snaps of your home or office, pets, neighborhood, church friends . . . New friends will enjoy seeing how you live.

Here are a few nuggets of practical wisdom for your tour of duty:

- On talking: Mind your tongue.
- On unsanitary conditions on the field: Use a knuckle, elbow, paper towel . . . Or use your foot.
- On foreign food: Even if you don't like it, don't make goop.
- On group activities: Whatever suits the rest.
- On sharing the good news of Jesus: Whoever gets *his* blood, they'll sure see a change!

PRAYER

Focus some time today on asking God to help you be a better listener. Then practice by listening to his still, small voice.

THINGS UNSEEN

This is a take-out devo.

Find a nice view of woods, mountains, a meadow, lake, or beach. If you can't get to a nature spot today, skip this devo until you can.

Grab a cup of coffee, your Bible, and a pencil. Draw in a deep breath and take a look around.

With just days before you hit the road—and way too much to do—you may be stressed. Cast all those cares on Jesus for a minute and think on him . . .

A crisis, some people explain, is merely condensed information. When simple duties like buying mouthwash and paying a bill begin to logjam, stress happens. Distribute the chores among the days remaining before your trip. Put essentials first.

Delegate. Pray about priorities. Write down the big things you have yet to do.

Look around you again. What's happening? Are trees moving in the breeze? Are insects buzzing? Is rain falling? What else? Describe the scene, the gentle grass, crystal snow, or quiet sand. Go ahead—get a little poetic.

Invisible Forces

Guess what else is going on? While you sit there fairly collected, gigantic, invisible forces are at work all around you. You can't see them or hear them.

But they're there, monstrous powers creating and destroying.

Miles beneath your feet lay molten oceans of churning, volcanic lava ready to burst forth. Tectonic plates press against each other with unimaginable stress, grinding and crushing, pressing until . . . *boom!* Earthquake.

But for now all is quiet.

If it's a clear morning, there will be dew dissolving, morning mists floating by, steam rising from your coffee. Peaceful? Hardly. From 93 million miles away, the sun's raw heat is lifting that moisture, drawing up massive clouds from sea and lake, pond and puddle. Look up. There it is: the atmosphere, 5.5 quadrillion tons of it, weight-lifted by the sun. How can such an incredible mass float over you and not crush you like a pancake while you sit and sip? That big, hulking atmosphere is working to keep more than 6.7 billion of us—and our planet—temperate and moist.

And who but a few sky nerds pays any attention?

If you're looking up at a clear night sky, the whole universe—hidden by day—is unmasked by darkness. You see billions of silent stars. But in every direction galaxies collide, stars implode, and black holes—if they do exist—swallow entire systems. You see and hear nothing of that. Only twinkling peace.

While you sit and take it all in, gargantuan systems are locked in, balanced, and working—and have been from the beginning—to make life possible on earth.

Held Together

Look around at the vegetation, unfolding so slowly the growth can't be seen. How unpretentiously do seedlings crack sidewalks to get to the sunlight! Vast, unseen networks of roots work their way down, unheard and unnoticed, digesting mountains of nutrients through the soil to make life. Megacities of insect life cultivate the earth. How quietly it all happens.

CULTURE

As magnificent as nature is, no wonder nature worshipers have always been found around the globe, mistakenly worshiping creation instead of its creator. Human sacrifices have been made to volcanoes and rivers. Mountains, waterfalls, and rocks may be considered gods. Even fruits and vegetables are venerated; instead of thanking God for the tomato, animists may thank the tomato for existing. And nature worship is not limited to ancient times; Wicca is seeing a revival.

Jesus is holding all nature together. "By him all things were created: things in heaven and on earth, visible and invisible, whether thrones or powers or rulers or authorities; all things were created by him and for him. He is before all things, and in him all things hold together" (Colossians 1:16, 17).

The more one understands about nature, the more power these verses pack. (And for the armchair scientist, a question: Sometimes I wonder . . . That mysterious, hypothetical force called dark energy that is omnipresent, supposedly comprises over 70 percent of the universe, and exerts a gravitational pull but does not emit or absorb light . . . Sometimes I wonder . . . Is that "dark energy" the hand of Jesus holding all things together?)

And the Holy Spirit is working. Moving through the world like a 5.5 quadrillion-ton wind, yet hardly noticed. Where you're going, he's already working.

When Jesus drew attention to creation—lilies of the field, birds of the air—to teach about God's presence and provision, his audience understood what he meant. Today we know a little more about the universe—of quarks and quasars and plate tectonics—but still, "How faint the whisper we hear of him! Who then can understand the thunder of his power?" (Job 26:14).

Much of what the Holy Spirit will do during your trip you'll never see: seeds of faith planted and germinating, rains of healing for parched souls, the Son's light shining in once-dark hearts. Faith is being "certain of what we do not see" (Hebrews 11:1). God is accomplishing a vast purpose he's had in mind since the foundation of the earth. And he's using you.

He may be reordering your little universe right now, heating things up. Stay calm. The Father oversees, the Spirit moves, the Son holds it all together. Thank him for that.

Finish off that coffee and go take on the day.

THERE'S A
NEW GOD IN TOWN

According to the October 16, 2007 *Time* article (www.time.com), there's a new god in town. Her name is Santa Muerte ("Saint Death"). Her worshipers dress her skeletal form in a death shroud or a kind of wedding dress. The new patron saint of Mexican drug lords has a growing number of followers in the general population.

A few years ago, Mark Northrup, missionary in Saltillo, Mexico, noticed shrines to her appearing on the roadsides, alongside statues of Mary. The death shrines now often outnumber and outsize the Mary shrines.

A small shrine to Santa Muerte, Northrup further explains, may occupy a corner of a room in a worshiper's house . . . at first. Then as the demands for more offerings increase—some devotees even claim to hear her voice—the shrine must grow: more flowers, more treats and drinks, until the entire house is swallowed up in offerings to holy death.

Some say that she is just Mary in skeleton form. Why portray Jesus' mother this way? No one seems to know; the roots of demonic cults are usually hard to trace, part of their appeal being their mysterious beginnings. There are ties to an Aztec goddess of the lowest realm of the Aztec underworld, ties to the powerful Mexican drug culture, and a spin-off of the Roman tradition of offerings and prayers to saints.

Some devotees of Saint Death have left the church; but others remain, worshiping her along with Mary and Jesus.

Creepy processions and prayers to a skeleton dressed in formal attire look macabre to most of us. But they are becoming all too familiar in northern Mexico and in a few U.S. cities.

In Your Zip Code?

There are other new gods in town. And many American believers are unaware of them, or naive to the fact that being "spiritual" isn't always necessarily a good thing. Though some find pagan religions exotic and interesting, we need to remember that certain areas of the spirit world are bad neighborhoods.

Have you ever encountered the dark side of religion, the worship of false gods? What happened?

Gods are immigrating across borders in hope of a better life: more worshipers, bigger offerings to spread their anti-gospel.

Western-style yoga is Hinduism repackaged. Old yogis, ragged and covered with the ashes of corpses, are replaced by young, trim health instructors in spandex. "A small army of yoga missionaries [has been trained to] set upon the Western world. They may not call themselves Hindu, but Hindus know where yoga came from and where it goes" (*Hinduism Today,* 01/19/91).

Krishna consciousness came to the States as Christ consciousness in the early 1900s. What does the term *Christ consciousness* mean? "Honor your self," said Swami Muktananda. "Worship your self, kneel to your self. God dwells within you as you" (www.hindu ismtoday.com).

Who's the new Hindu god in town? You are.

And this happened in Bloomington, Indiana, on March 29, 2006: "The monks of the Tibetan Cultural Center performed a special fire prayer. The purpose . . . was to purify the grounds and to request the local deities for continued spiritual support" (www.tibetancc.com).

Local Deities?

The Dalai Lama, god-king of tantric (black magic/ sex magic) Tibetan Buddhism, is a wildly popular world leader. To many people he seems to be a spiritual leader filled with great wisdom and compassion. A little googling, however, will uncover the use of skull bowls, human thighbone trumpets, demonic rites in cemeteries, and mandala rituals performed in the U.S. to take mystic possession of our land.

Pretty heavy stuff. There are people who aren't even sure that demons exist. But I've spoken with Christian workers from Benin, Jamaica, China, Mexico, Korea, Venezuela, Ghana . . . and Kentucky who have no doubts. What has been your experience?

TRAVEL

You know the *real* God. What a privilege to be able to carry his message! Take along the gospel story in a way that anyone can understand, regardless of age or language. The gospel in cartoon format, colored bracelet or wordless book, gospel story cubes . . . Use them as the occasion presents itself and give them away when appropriate.

On Your Guard

A brief Scripture primer before you go:

1. False gods are fiction, but the power behind them is demonic. They may appear and reappear

under different disguises. "They . . . angered [God] with their detestable idols. They sacrificed to demons, which are not God—gods they had not known, *gods that recently appeared*, gods your fathers did not fear (Deuteronomy 32:16, 17, emphasis added; see also 1 Corinthians 10:20).

2. False gods make people do crazy things. "They worshiped their idols, which became a snare to them. They sacrificed their sons and their daughters to demons" (Psalm 106:36, 37).

3. Even repeating their names may be spiritually dangerous. "Do not invoke the names of other gods; do not let them be heard on your lips" (Exodus 23:13).

4. Jesus effectively used the Word to defeat Satan (Matthew 4:1-11).

PRAYER

Seek God's truth about the nature of satanic activity in the area to which you will be traveling. Then pray for God's protection!

5. Jesus kept conversations with demons to a minimum (Luke 4:4, 8, 12, 35; Mark 5:8, 9).

6. Jesus' followers knew the difference between demonization and illness (Matthew 4:24, 25; Luke 9:1).

7. Devils know and fear God. "What do you want with us, Jesus of Nazareth? Have you come to destroy us? I know who you are—the Holy One of God!" (Luke 4:34).

8. Satan may have geographic headquarters somewhere on earth. "I know where you live—where Satan has his throne . . . where Satan lives" (Revelation 2:13).

9. Ultimately there is "eternal fire prepared for the devil and his angels" (Matthew 25:41; see Jude 6; 2 Peter 2:4).

10. Insidiously clever "doctrines of devils" will be accepted by unwary Christians (1 Timothy 4:1, *KJV*). In *The Dust of Death*, Os Guinness says it well: "The subtlety of Eastern religion is that it enters like an odorless poison gas, seeping under the door, through the keyhole, in through open

windows, so that the man in the room is over-come without his ever realizing there was any danger at all" (www.firstcenturychristian.com).

New gods are in town, but there's a whiff of ancient decay about them. Pray for discernment.

BEING INTENTIONAL?

Intentional is a popular buzzword among Christians nowadays. We're supposed to be intentional about our faith, naturally. But when working in a strange, unfamiliar place with strange, unfamiliar people, intentionality may spell trouble.

Among your list of good intentions on the mission field may be to: always say and do the right thing, never have a bad hair day, be Jesus-like, be attractive on much less sleep, not get sick, be admired by everyone, do something big and flashy for God, and storm the gates of Hell.

Those are good intentions, pretty much my short-termer list. And though I haven't entirely given up on my list—even the shallower points about good hair and being admired—I've added a few things: get comfortable with my own stupidity, try not to embarrass my country, be happy to take the backseat, offer to stay behind to do grunge work, and be willing to eat that thing with feet and feathers on my plate.

Good Intentions Are Fine, But . . .

During a two-year stint overseas teaching English-Bible, my daughter had been trying to have a positive effect on a certain businessman in her class. Finally, her opportunity came: an invitation from his wife for dinner at their house. My daughter intended to talk about the Lord, to discuss the Bible, to have an enjoyable time.

The wife hogged the conversation—in her native language—speaking too fast and furious to be understood. Beer was served. Custom dictates that it would be *very* rude to refuse, so my daughter took a few polite sips even though she isn't a beer drinker. She understood little of the one-sided discussion, only nodding agreement where it seemed she might be supposed to. The evening felt like a total waste of time.

"I wanted to share Christ with my student," she said later. "But it didn't happen. I had to keep telling myself, 'OK, just smile and nod and drink your beer.'"

Jesus' Intentionality

What you intend for the best may not happen. Not that you should be purposeless; Jesus acted intentionally. He had a plan from the foundation of the earth: fulfilling all Scripture and saving the world (see Luke 19:10).

But he spent a lot of time just hanging out with people who wouldn't listen to him. Can you see Jesus with gluttons, blabbermouths, prostitutes, winebibbers—taking a few sips while the lot of them got blind drunk and acted ridiculously, hogging the conversation? Their idea of a great evening may have been to show off for the famous rabbi so they could brag the next day, "Guess who was at my house last night—that new teacher from Galilee! We sure showed him a good time. We trashed the place!"

Imagine Jesus nodding, smiling, sipping wine, sitting at a rowdy table of the great unwashed, listening as they went on and on about their lives . . . when he, God incarnate, had the very words of life to offer. If only they'd listen.

CULTURE

Jesus waited with infinite patience for his opportunities. With nonbelievers one must be longsuffering.

They don't know the Lord, so they may not recognize him in you. And they may press some unwelcome customs on you. Handle with grace.

Jesus spent long hours with people so they would eventually listen. He worked miracles to woo them into his presence so they could receive his love, his words of life. After the feeding of the five thousand, crowds came back the next day—not for words but for free food. But those whose ears were primed to hear, primed by Jesus' kindness, eventually got it.

Jesus' intention was not to be a one-man fast-food drive-through. His focus was to bring grace. In the end he would even set aside a most primal instinct—to stay alive—for that goal of grace. He endured what he hated to achieve what he loved. That is, he endured the cross to achieve our redemption.

Adapt

What are some of your intentions? Bring one person to Jesus? Get souvenirs for the fam? Take good pics for a presentation back home? Make ten new friends?

Wake up at the crack o' dawn every morning for quiet time? Pencil in two or three.

Be ready to cross off a few items or to write off the whole list if the Lord has something else in mind. God's plans are the best-laid plans. And you might fit into those plans in a different way than you intended.

CULTURE

You may have to take a sip of a foul beverage, sit on the floor when you'd like to have a chair, work when you need sleep. You may have to obey dumb instructions, go days without bathing, refrain from scowling at people as they bow to idols, wash dishes (in cold water!) when you thought you were going to be evangelizing. Adapt as needed.

Humble yourself like Isaiah.

Grieve like Paul.

Stand firm like Elijah.

Lead like Deborah.

Stay calm like Daniel.

Step forward like Esther.

Encourage like Barnabas.

Praise like David.

Scratch out the word *intentional* from this devo title. In its place write *flexible* or *adaptable*. Or *teachable*, which means "willing to change."

PRAYER

Talk to God today about these specific words: *intentional, flexible, adaptable, and teachable.*

"I know the plans I have for you," God said (Jeremiah 29:11). Just a thought: If the road to Hell is paved with good intentions, maybe the road to Heaven is paved with making the best of it when all your good intentions seem to get stomped on.

A CHAIN OF EVENTS

In the first devo, you considered your call to your upcoming mission. Now take some time to go back further, to think about your call to Christ for the long haul. Skim your whole life for those determining points and persons who influenced you over the years to serve the Lord. You may need to jot things down on scrap paper before you put them in order in your journal. Go all the way back to the first time you knew God was real.

What Happened?

Elijah the prophet. The guy showed up on the political stage loaded for bear, meaning he was firing the big gun with the big bullets for big game. "Now Elijah . . . said to Ahab, 'As the LORD, the God of Israel, lives, whom I serve, there will be neither dew nor rain in the next few years except at my word'" (1 Kings 17:1).

Then the word of the Lord came to Elijah: "Now run! Run like the wind!" (loose translation). God did warn Elijah to quickly go hide in Kerith Ravine, where ravens would feed him. As sun parched the land and the bad news sank in, King Ahab sent out spies. "There is not a nation or kingdom where [Ahab] has not sent someone to look for you" (18:10). No doubt Ahab wanted to bring Elijah into the royal torture chamber and squeeze some precipitation out of him. Elijah could have had the shortest ministry on record: a one-verse sermon.

Have you ever wondered how Elijah was forged into a fiery prophet? One just doesn't wake up one morning and say, "I think I'll go to the capitol, pronounce national disaster by God's power, and bring it to pass— all alone." Something had to have happened to him long before that, something that cultivated his extreme faith and tested his courage. Was it trauma and tragedy? confrontation with dark forces? miracles?

Culture Happens

Though we know nothing of the prophet Elijah's beginnings, we do know quite a bit about his culture. It was approximately 800 BC. Israel had sunk into idolatry. Wimpy King Ahab had married pagan, evangelistic Jezebel, daughter of King Ethbaal of the Sidonians (16:31). Jezebel had imported a battalion of ascetic priests into Israel and killed every religious leader of Yahweh worship she could find. True devotion to God was disappearing from the face of the earth.

Enter Elijah. Certainly he'd heard news of the religious executions, of faith dying out. His friend Obadiah had hidden fellow prophets in caves. Read the whole story in 1 Kings 17, 18. We won't know until we sit down for a long talk in Heaven what events built Elijah's character or when he first knew God was truly real. I can't wait to ask him!

Your Alpha Point

The fictional teen Elijah Creek described his alpha

point this way: "It's hard to say when I started to really believe in God. I guess I knew from when I was four years old down in Georgia and woke up in the middle of the night for no reason. I went out to the porch just in time to see lightning strike a tree. I kind of knew I was supposed to see it, so it didn't scare me. I didn't run inside and wake Mom—I never told anyone. Maybe it was him saying to me even way back then: *Know who you're dealing with, Elijah Creek*" (*The Haunted Soul* by Lena Wood).

Connect the dots of your life—those points of change—all the way back to the alpha point, the very first memory you have that God was real. What do you remember?

I was six years old. I woke up one night during an electrical storm, scared but not wanting to wake up

Mommy and Daddy. So I kept talking to God until it went away. And there was another point back further, one that I don't even remember. I was only two the first time my sister and I sang in church. Someone stood us up in front of the assembly, and we sang the old hymn "Sing the Wondrous Love":

> *Sing the wondrous love of Jesus,*
> *Sing His mercy and His grace;*
> *In the mansions bright and blessed,*
> *He'll prepare for us a place.*
> *While we walk the pilgrim pathway*
> *Clouds will overspread the sky;*
> *But when trav'ling days are over,*
> *Not a shadow, not a sigh.*
> *When we all get to heaven!*
> *What a day of rejoicing that will be!*
> *When we all see Jesus,*
> *We'll sing and shout the victory.*

Surely God was speaking to and calling my little heart as I sang. But who knew this beloved hymn by Eliza Hewitt would become a reflection of our entire family's pilgrimage? Over the years every one of us has had trav'ling days—as short- or long-termers, an international nanny, a gypsy for Jesus. Our pilgrim pathway—probably like yours—has been overshadowed with clouds: health problems, financial disasters, divorce . . . even an untimely death when my brother-in-law came home three weeks into a mission trip and died soon after. At his funeral, hundreds joyfully sang and shouted this victory song, stunning our nonbeliever friends.

PRAYER

Spend some time with your Father, thanking him for the chain of events and people he has used to bring you this far.

TRAVEL

You may become an important "dot" that helps someone on this trip connect to Jesus. Before your trip, buy two of some small item, one for yourself and one to give away. Suggestions: key ring, pen, mug, notebook, magnet, collectible . . . Share this little gift with a special friend you meet. Tell the person that you have an item exactly like this and want him/her to have a matching one—as a memento of your time together.

When you connect the dots in your life, you may be surprised to see that string of seemingly random events—some good, some bad—begin to look like a well-orchestrated plan that forged you and brought you to this place. And this is just the beginning. "No eye has seen, no ear has heard, no mind has conceived what God has prepared for those who love him" (1 Corinthians 2:9).

PILGRIMAGE, PART 1

Holy Places?

The term *pilgrimage* typically refers to a sacred journey to a sacred place.

Islam has its hajj to Mecca. Muslims circle the Kaaba seven times and kiss the Black Stone as a focal point of their worship of Allah.

Shrines and guided tours abound in Israel for Jews, Christians, and Muslims. Visit Capernaum, the Sea of Galilee, Jerusalem. Hear conflicting reports by tour guides:

"Jesus died here."

"No, here!"

"He was buried here."

"No, here!"

If the Garden of Eden is ever found, people will flock to it in droves. Entrepreneurs will set up shop, selling fig leaves, snake jewelry, and postcards. Tiny T-shirts will say, "Grandma went to the Garden of Eden, and all I got was a lousy apple." There'll be photo ops where you can stick your head into a life-size painting of a naked couple, their crucial areas hidden by shrubs. Yes, they'll pave paradise and put in a Mickey D's.

Buddhists make pilgrimages to the Bodhi Tree, Deer Park, and Vulture Peak. Guided tours are reasonably priced. A few finger bones—the remains of Buddha's cremation twenty-five hundred years ago—are now objects of veneration and on tour themselves. Pilgrims accompany them and pray in their presence.

Roman Catholics adopted a similar practice, hosting relic sites around the world. Of note is the recent exhumation of Padre Pio, dead forty years but listed in "fair condition" by church officials. Large numbers of pilgrims are expected to pray at his remains throughout the time the body is on display (www.wikipedia.org).

Through city streets in Japan, Shinto worshipers carry portable deity shrines that are strikingly similar to the ark of the covenant. Some world religions still have God in a box.

Hindus have the Ganges River for washing away sins—though the fecal level is 1.5 million times the safe level for drinking (*U.S. News & World Report*, 11/26/07).

New Agers convene at power spots of Gaia (earth goddess) around the world: Machu Picchu in Peru, Glastonbury in the U.K., Ayers Rock in Australia, and Arizona's Sedona area.

Old Testament occultists had their groves and high places too, their idols and magic objects. It's nothing new.

How about you? Are there any places you have considered sacred? Have you ever been on pilgrimage? Describe those occasions.

Jacob's Pilgrimage

The patriarch Jacob said to Pharaoh, "The years of my pilgrimage are a hundred and thirty. My years have been few and difficult, and they do not equal the years of the pilgrimage of my fathers" (Genesis 47:9).

Jacob was not speaking of treks to holy places, but of his pilgrim life. He was a stay-at-home guy until he stole his brother Esau's birthright. He fled to Uncle Laban's farm. On the way, he dreamed of a ladder to Heaven. The Lord spoke, "I am with you and will watch over you wherever you go" (28:15). That spot became a holy place to Jacob; he called it Bethel, "house of God."

Where and how have you encountered God in a dramatic way?

Jacob's Uncle Laban devised a conspiracy for Jacob's wedding night that resulted in contentious sister-wives and years of family tension for Jacob. Laban grew hostile to Jacob's success. Time to go. Later on his journey he was met by angels (32:1).

Jacob sent word to his long-estranged brother, wanting to reconcile. Word came back: Esau is coming—with four hundred men! That night Jacob wrestled with a messenger of the Lord and named that place Peniel, the "face of God" (32:22-32).

On the Road Again

Jacob lived beyond the Jordan, then moved to a new place and called it El Elohe Israel, "mighty is the God of Israel" (33:20). Once again, trouble came. Rape and revenge. God said, "Go back to Bethel." Jacob renamed it El Bethel, "God of the house of God" (35:7).

Again he moved. At Ephrath his beloved Rachel died. He pitched his tent beyond Migdal Eder. In his old age, Jacob went to Egypt to confirm that his long-lost son Joseph was alive. When Jacob died, his bones made one last trip back to Canaan for burial. The homeboy made it home at age 147 (47:28-30; 50:12, 13).

Do you see? In a Jacob-style pilgrimage, there was trouble all along the way. And God kept showing up—in every place. Jacob's family was flawed, but God was faithful. Your saintly pilgrimage will have nothing to do with holy boxes, bones, idols, or power spots. You'll be walking with God wherever you go.

PRAYER

As you meet God at holy places (in other words, everywhere), pray that you will be receptive to his words. Commit to obeying his commands. He promises to be with you.

PILGRIMAGE, PART 2

Hebrew 11:13-16 says that the Old Testament greats "were still living by faith when they died. . . . They admitted that they were aliens and strangers [*pilgrims*] on earth. . . . They were longing for a better country—a heavenly one. Therefore God is not ashamed to be called their God, for he has prepared a city for them."

The word *pilgrim* comes from the Latin *peregrinus*. *Peregrine falcon* means "wandering hawk." In aerial gymnastic/ballet/dive-bombing style, these raptors can plunge from tremendous heights at up to 140 miles per hour. They are the fastest animals on the planet, the most widespread birds of prey in the world, living everywhere except the coldest arctic climates. They soar and dive fearlessly. They keep a keen eye.

The Peregrini

Patrick of Ireland and those who followed in his wake became known as the Irish peregrini. From around AD 400 onward they carried the gospel to the four corners of Ireland, and from there throughout

Europe, taking on the culture (or lack thereof) of wild Pict tribal peoples, warring Gauls, and druid priests. They confronted the power of kings and the spiritual poverty of the masses (www.urbana.org).

Patrick understood both sides of Jacob's patriarchal pilgrimage: the hostility and the hope. Murchiú, a seventh-century historian, wrote on the life of Patrick and included this prophecy by druids against him (quoted here from www.petermanseye.com):

> *Across the sea will come Adze-head,*
> *crazed in the head,*
> *his cloak with hole for the head,*
> *his stick bent in the head.*
> *He will chant impieties from a table*
> *in the front of his house;*
> *all his people will answer: "so be it, so be it."*

Like Jacob, Patrick met with antagonism in strange places. And like Jacob, Patrick was also aware of spiritual protection. He wrote a poem/prayer that has come to be called his breastplate. It begins (quoted here from www.christianitytoday.com):

I arise today
Through a mighty strength, the invocation of the Trinity,
Through the belief in the Threeness,
Through confession of the Oneness
Of the Creator of creation.

Toward the end of the prayer, Patrick reveals his awareness of God's presence:

Christ with me, Christ before me, Christ behind me,
Christ in me, Christ beneath me, Christ above me,
Christ on my right, Christ on my left . . .

Compose your own prayer/poem about God's presence for the days ahead.

TRAVEL

Jesus' light is the most important item you'll take on your mission trip. But a bandanna—though not nearly as valuable—will come in pretty handy too. It can protect an injury, protect the mouth and nose from dust, protect the head from heat . . . Use it as a tourniquet, a sweatband, a washcloth, a syphon, as tinder to burn, as a signal flag to wave. Keep a sunburn cooled with water, carry things in it, wipe up spills, fold it as a potholder, cover a hole in the sole of your shoe . . . A fun idea is for all members of your team to wear bandannas, choosing colors to indicate sub-teams: green for the money-keepers, blue for the drama/music people, yellow for the laundry crew . . . And if appropriate, let each person take along some extras of his color to give as gifts to new friends.

Although facts about the peregrini are mixed with fable, their stories have endured:

Brendan, the legendary Irish voyager, and a band of adventurers set out on the Atlantic without sail or oar, letting God steer their craft. There are wild speculations that he could have been the first European to reach

America, nearly a thousand years before Christopher Columbus (www.prayerfoundation.org).

Columba, also called Columcille, was strong, evangelistic, and hot-tempered (like his namesake Mel Columcille Gibson). He founded dozens of Christian communities in Ireland, then Iona. From there he went to Scotland. He was described as an example in study and prayer.

Aidan evangelized England.

Columbanus began there and went on to Germany, France, and Italy.

There were scores of others. Distressed by the immorality of church leaders and believers in Europe, these Irish pilgrims led them to repent anew. They preached, baptized, and ordained wherever they pleased, regardless of the hierarchical authority of Rome. Some went solo, some in teams; others were married. They shone light into Europe's Dark Age from AD 400 to 950.

The peregrini would find a location, build a simple meeting room, classrooms, and lodging. Once a community was established, some went on to new fields, others stayed behind as builders and teachers.

They learned the local language, translated the Bible, and wrote out hymns. They trained small groups of young men as interns. Instead of attacking the deception in others' religion, they preached the truth of the gospel and let God's Word and his Spirit do the unmasking. They taught salvation by faith in Jesus (www.urbana.org).

This poem, ascribed to Aidan, reflects the two waves of your upcoming trip: going solo to commune with God and going out to the world:

> *Leave me alone with God as much as may be.*
> *As the tide draws the waters close in upon the shore,*
> *Make me an island, set apart, alone with you,*
> *God, holy to you.*
> *Then with the turning of the tide,*
> *Prepare me to carry your presence*
> *to the busy world beyond,*
> *The world that rushes in on me till the waters*
> *come again and fold me back to you.*

PRAYER

Meditate with God today on these two concepts: going solo with him and going out into the world.

A Pilgrim Song

A few years ago a manuscript estimated to be at least one thousand years old was found in a bog in the midlands of Ireland. About twenty vellum pages were recovered. Named the Faddan More Psalter from the location where it was found, it was probably created by monks as early as AD 800. Bogs were often used for hiding valuables, especially during Viking raids. A medieval psalter with ornately decorated pages would have required hundreds of man-hours to produce. Interestingly, when discovered, the psalter was opened to Psalm 84, a song of pilgrimage (www.wikipedia.org).

Like the falcon, the Irish peregrini lived far and wide. They were perhaps the most wide-spreading mission movement of their age. They soared to the heights of devotion and plunged into struggle and sacrifice. They were fast and fearless. And they kept a keen eye on God.

PILGRIMAGE, PART 3

This question was asked on answers.yahoo.com: "Christians: What are some encouraging verses that I can give to a person who is on dialysis?" The suffering person had lost joy. The chosen Best Answer was Psalm 84:

¹How lovely is your dwelling place, O LORD Almighty!

²My soul yearns, even faints, for the courts of the LORD; my heart and my flesh cry out for the living God.

³Even the sparrow has found a home, and the swallow a nest for herself, where she may have her young—a place near your altar, O LORD Almighty, my King and my God.

⁴Blessed are those who dwell in your house; they are ever praising you. Selah.

⁵Blessed are those whose strength is in you, who have set their hearts on pilgrimage.

⁶As they pass through the Valley of Baca, they make it a place of springs; the autumn rains also cover it with pools.

⁷They go from strength to strength, till each appears before God in Zion.

⁸Hear my prayer, O LORD God Almighty; listen to me, O God of Jacob. Selah.

⁹Look upon our shield, O God; look with favor on your anointed one.

¹⁰Better is one day in your courts than a thousand elsewhere; I would rather be a doorkeeper in the house of my God than dwell in the tents of the wicked.

¹¹For the LORD God is a sun and shield; the LORD bestows favor and honor; no good thing does he withhold from those whose walk is blameless.

¹²O LORD Almighty, blessed is the man who trusts in you.

Psalm 84 recounts making a journey to the temple of God. The poet yearns to be near the Lord, suggesting that even birds build their nests around the temple to be close to their creator. Look online at some YouTube performances of "How Lovely is Your Dwelling Place" written by Arnel Aquino, or "How Lovely is Thy Dwelling Place" from *Requiem* by Brahms—beautiful songs based on this three-thousand-year-old psalm.

CULTURE

The impact of the Bible worldwide can hardly be argued. Reports vary, but one source says that the Bible has been translated into 2,212 of the world's 6,500 languages (www.biblesociety.org).

The Place Where God Dwells

In Psalm 84:2 the writer speaks as if he has been prevented from the temple, but now he's thrilled to be returning to the place where the Lord dwells.

In verses 3 and 4 the psalmist moves back to prayer. The swallow and sparrow—and we might add, the peregrine falcon—build their nests in cathedrals and temples. The poet understands how blessed are the priests and Levites who have rooms near the sanctuary.

Verses 5-7 speak of pilgrimage. The highway of the pilgrim is in the heart.

Is the Valley of Baca in verse 6 a literal dry valley on the way to Jerusalem, a symbol of spiritual dryness, or even a symbol of spiritual warfare? Whatever the meaning, the valley comes to life as pilgrims pass through it. The wandering saint gains strength on the journey. The goal is not getting to a temple—a building with altars—but to be near God.

In verse 9 the psalmist speaks of "our shield," perhaps referring both to the anointed king and the coming Messiah.

PRAYER

Verse 10 (restated in your own words) would be a great motto for your mission as you are called upon to serve in a variety of ways. Speak these words back to God in your time with him today.

The psalmist concludes by speaking of sun and shield, depicting life source and protector. Blessings of life and peace come to those who love to spend time with the Lord, who trust in him.

Of all the names and symbols for God in this psalm, which speaks the most about your relationship with him? Why is that?

The Real Temple

In the New Testament, Jesus makes it clear to the Samaritan woman that real worship doesn't need a central temple (John 4). It never did. The great people of faith met God in the wilderness, in their homes, all along the way. Worship happens in spirit and in truth. We are the temple now, the sacred place where the Holy Spirit dwells.

Paul said that Jesus "came and preached peace to you who were far away and peace to those who were near. For through him we both have access to the

Father by one Spirit. Consequently, you are no longer foreigners and aliens, but fellow citizens with God's people and members of God's household" (Ephesians 2:17-19).

The online Best Answer of Psalm 84 was a good one, wasn't it? Whether you're hospital-bound because of dialysis or mission-bound with a backpack slung over your shoulder, these are encouraging verses. The highway's in your heart. So pilgrim, you are not wandering to sacred spaces. You know your destination. In one sense you're already there. You are in Christ, and he is in you.

LOOKING FOR A SAVIOR

Let's take one more glimpse at world religions, this time through another lens. Do a little snooping on the Web (at places like www.falsemessiahs.com or the occult site www.iamuniversity.ch) or at the library, and you'll turn up a surprise. It seems there are more messiahs out there waiting to manifest than you can shake a stick at.

Muslims (especially Shia and Sufi branches) believe that Mahdi, the last imam, will prepare the way for the second coming of . . . Jesus? That's right. And Muslims believe that Christians and Jews who convert at the end times will become part of the global Islamic religion.

The Buddhist messiah is Maitreya, the Buddha of the future. Plans are currently being made to build a gargantuan statue of this Planetary Christ, an idol designed to last one thousand years (www.indianskyscraperblog.wordpress.com).

To the Hindus, the coming Kalki Avatar will appear on a white horse as an incarnation of Vishnu. Some Hindus equate him with Jesus. Pantheists (who believe that everything is God) are often willing to include Jesus as a messiah—believing that the more gods, the better.

Have you ever met someone who believed in a messiah who isn't Jesus? How did your conversation go?

i mean.... seriously. get out more.

Many Messiahs?

For Christians, Jesus is God incarnate and the only Redeemer. At the end of time he will return; all creation will be recycled into "a new heaven and a new earth" (Revelation 21:1). Satan and his works will be destroyed (20:7-10).

In Aztec/Mayan teaching Quetzalcoatl (a feathered serpent) is a deity. His "return to earth" is disputed. This messianic myth resembles other Native American legends, especially Sioux (a man from the East in a red cloak will come) and Hopi (Pahana, the "true white brother" will come from the East, wearing a red cap and cloak).

Rastafarians believe that Haile Selassie was God incarnate.

The founder of the Baha'i faith, Baha'u'llah, claimed that he was the returning Christ, the embodiment of Jesus, but also the fulfillment of prophecies of other religions as well.

Orthodox Jews believe a Messiah will come to return God's glory to Jerusalem.

The Zoroastrian Savior is Saoshyant, who will restore all things.

And there are at least ten people living today who have claimed to be Jesus or Christ—among them Sun Myung Moon, Charles Manson, and José Luis de Jesús Miranda.

The True Messiah

The real, historic Jesus seems to get lost in the shuffle, doesn't he? He warned us it would be this way. "Watch out that no one deceives you. For many will come in my name, claiming, 'I am the Christ,' and will deceive many" (Matthew 24:4, 5).

There are other messiah-like titles floating around these days, including "the christ-thing which has no name." A messiah-thing? What is *that*? Perhaps this title really hints at the popular (and spreading like wildfire) concept of Christ consciousness (also called the Buddha nature, goddess within, self-divinity). As one New Ager explains, "The Aquarian Age will make us aware that each human being is a messiah unto himself" (www.deoxy.org). What a scary world where each one is his own final authority! We're back to square one, aren't we—when the evil one suggested, "You will be like God" (Genesis 3:5).

CULTURE

In the place you're going, are they looking for a messiah? Or have they been taught to believe that each one must save himself by his own works? Or maybe they believe there is nothing to be saved *from*, that no messiah is even necessary.

Spend time today thinking about the real, living Christ, the one whom every heart is deeply yearning for. Though multitudes around the world know him, billions still wait. This song, written the day before 9/11, expresses how much the world needs Jesus!

The Fall of Man
by Andrea Summer

I get myself down, get lost in what's around
I lose the joy I had, wonder why everything feels so bad
And I bury my face, lose my mind and lose my faith
And right before I hit the ground I hear,
"Don't forget my saving grace."
O God, you warned me it would be this way
This is my life when I choose to turn away
But this isn't what you meant for my life. . . .
Timothy McVeigh died the other day
And a woman drowned her children in the tub
An accidental killing started riots on the streets
And if you ask me, our hearts are getting numb
Open your eyes, he warned us it would be this way
This is life when half the world is turned away
But this isn't what he meant for our lives
O world, believe him, for to take these sins and set us free
He sent his perfect Sacrifice to bleed

O world seek him, 'cause he's all you've ever
wanted and more
O how we need a Savior
You know you need him,
in the midst of all this dying and war
O how the world needs a Savior.

PRAYER

Dear Jesus, our Messiah, we need you. As we go out on pilgrimage, may we take your name in power, your Word as a sword, and your holiness as a shield. Help us to show others that we care. Help us to listen first, to earn the right to be heard. May your love and light shine through us. Amen.

ABOUT THE AUTHOR

Lena Wood has a lifelong history of missions and writing. She has been on mission trips to Japan five times, has been involved in homeless ministry and children's ministry at her church in Kentucky, and maintains contact and prayer support for missionaries all over the world. A former editor at Standard Publishing, she has written articles, skits, songs, programs, and curriculum, as well as the seven-book youth fiction series Elijah Creek & The Armor of God (www.standardpub.com). Lena is an artist, a worship leader, and the mother of two grown daughters, Arian and Andrea.

www.lenawood.com